SEO 2014

Includes How to Recover From Penguin, Panda or Manual Penalties

By Darren Varndell

EZ Website Promotion Volume 4
2014 Paperback Edition

Copyright, Legal Notice and Disclaimer

Table of Contents

INTRODUCTION

SEO - *Search Engine Optimization* is the term given to obtaining traffic for your website from "organic" free listings in search engine result pages (SERPS). Google, Yahoo and Bing all show these pages when a user enters a search term or phrase into a search box located on one of these search engines. The key to search optimization, and tapping into this free traffic, is to get your website listed as high as possible in these search pages for keyword(s) related to your company or business.

SEO refers to the various tasks involved in making a website and web pages search engine friendly in order to ensure high rankings and the traffic it brings. With the largest search engine, Google, using in excess of two hundred signals to decide upon a websites topic and relevance, the world of SEO can seem a daunting area at first. However, not all of these signals are equal, with this manual cutting through the minefield of search optimization and presenting some insight into the most critical areas of SEO that need to be addressed on your website, concentrating on the main aspects that produce the best results and biggest impact on your search engine *rankings* (the position your site appears in search results).

2013 was an interesting year with regards to search optimization. A range of updates from major search engines signaled a new dawn, where simply pointing thousands of unrelated links, using keywords as anchor text, at a website to make it rank on the first page of results not only met an abrupt end, but could also get your website penalized, or worse still, removed from the index altogether.

In the first section of this book we will discuss healthy and effective SEO practices to help your website rank higher, and avoid penalties that could be placed on your site for a breach of the search engine rules and guidelines.

Later in this book we examine recent important search engine updates that could have had (or will have) a negative impact on your website rankings, along with corrective strategies.

Finally we look at identifying and recovering from manual actions that could be placed against your website by Google's web spam team if you or someone working on your behalf (SEO consultant etc) has employed unethical *black hat* techniques in the past.

Now, more than ever, *on-page* search optimization is critical to obtaining high search rankings, alongside quality content and the end-user experience.

See the *Other Books* section for more in depth publications and SEO strategies. Also join our mailing list via the following link below for free SEO tips and tricks:

http://www.ezwebsitepromotion.com/newsletter/

FREE BONUS - Join our newsletter today and receive our traffic boosting e-book '*Top 10 SEO Tips*' absolutely FREE!

EFFECTIVE SEO

In order to tap in to this incredible flow of free website visitors from search engines it is necessary to construct (or edit) our website to make it *Search Engine Friendly.* By placing certain vital information (keywords) in the right quantities, into various locations within our website, we can help search engines identify the topic of our site, with the aim of positioning our website within the first few results shown when a user searches for our type of product or service.

For example, if we were marketing a website for a Pizza delivery business based in the New York area, we would want to be found within the first few results on major search engines when a user searches for a phrase such as; *'New York pizza delivery'.*

Reaching the number one position on search results pages for a relevant search will ensure a steady stream of *free targeted* visitors to your website, all ready for you to turn them into sales.

This section will help your website to achieve better search results by walking you through various elements and aspects of your website design that may require some modification or attention in order to achieve better search engine rankings, all without the risk of sanctions or other penalties for using techniques frowned upon my the major search engines.

Search engine optimization is most effective when you create unique, quality, compelling content for your website that also contains your related keywords. When you adopt this strategy you not only boost your rankings but provide more value for your website visitors.

If you create great quality content other people will want to link to it, either from relevant websites or related blogs, or by sharing it on social networks. This provides a stream of free traffic, in addition to sending search engines all the right signals.

Changes you make to your website can take some time to be updated by search engines, sometimes running into weeks. Be patient and wait for search engines to crawl through your site, obtain the updated information and index it correctly within its database(s).

Domain Names

A *domain name* (e.g. example.com) is a name used to identify a particular website on the internet. What this name actually represents is the numeric IP (Internet Protocol) address of a web server containing the actual files making up a website.

All devices on the internet connect to each other using these IP addresses. When you type a web address into a browser to visit a website, the browser automatically looks up the correct IP address for the server using DNS (a directory associating internet names with numbers) and seeks the web page from the web server located at the returned address.

You will need a domain name to identify your new website on the Internet. You can register these names via a domain registrar, in addition to most web hosting companies offering this as a service. After selecting a name you should use the registrars search service to verify it has not already been taken and is available to be registered by yourself.

When choosing a domain name think carefully about how relevant it is to your niche or business, how memorable it may be for people searching for your business or brand, and how complicated it may be for users to type into a web browser.

You should also try to include one or two of your *keywords* within your domain name (e.g. bobscarparts.com) but *do not* seek to register a domain name that *exactly* matches one of your main keyword phrases (e.g. usedcarparts.com).

This once effective SEO strategy was used to game search engines in the past, and in the case of competitive keywords, thanks to changes in search algorithms such as Google's

EMD (*Exact Match Domain*) update, could result in a penalty for your website.

After you have chosen, registered, and set-up a suitable domain name for your website, as directed by your web hosting provider, and once DNS servers have updated to reflect your new information, you are ready to go ahead and start creating the actual content for your site and uploading the pages that make up your website to your web server.

Page Title Tags

The HTML *title* tag is used within your page source code to assign a title to each individual page on your website. These tags provide information that is used by a web browser to display the page title, usually in the browsers main title bar, or alternatively within the tab in the case of a tabbed browser.

Search engines also use the information within your title to help classify your page, often using it as the clickable text part of your entry when your page is displayed in search engine result pages.

The contents of your title tag for each page plays a major role with regards to search engine ranking. Optimizing these tags for search will give you a boost in rankings on its own and so should not be overlooked. Optimize the title tags for each of your web pages, as described below, before moving on to other items in this checklist.

Create unique title tags for each page on your site. Each page on your site should have its own distinct title that is unique throughout your site.

Use brief, but descriptive titles that accurately describe the page's content. Include your keywords first and then your site name, as in the examples below:

Examples:

<title>keyword1 keyword2 keyword3 - sitename</title>

<title>1992 MX5 Wing Mirror – Bobs Car Parts</title>

The title tag should be placed within the *head* section of your page, between the opening *<head>* and closing *</head>* tags as shown below;

```
<html>
<head>
<title>Example Web Page Title</title>
</head>
<body>
...
</body>
</html>
```

Use 70 characters or less for your title tags as longer titles will be truncated by search engines in most cases. It is important to include relevant keywords for the page, but do not repeat keywords more than twice within a page title.

Refrain from the use of all uppercase characters within your page title and avoid the use of strange or unusual symbols.

Remember to make sure each page title is unique within the scope of your website, contains your keywords, and is relevant to the contents of the page.

Description Meta Tag

Each individual web page should have a HTML *meta-description* tag, again located within the *<head>* section of your page, describing the actual content contained on the page. This description text is often used in search engine result pages (SERPs) to describe the page within results, and usually shown beneath your page title in search listings.

As with page titles, search engines may use this information to help classify the content or topic of the page, and so should be considered a major ranking factor. You should ensure that all your web pages have unique, relevant and search optimized meta-description tags before moving on to the next item in this checklist.

Example:

<meta name="description" content="Click to buy MX5 wings mirrors and other great parts via our online store. Huge discounts at Bobs parts!">

The description tag should be placed within the head section of your page, i.e. between the <head> and </head> tags as shown in the example below;

<html>
<head>
<title>Example Page Title</title>
<meta name="description" content="Example Description">
</head>
<body>
...
</body>
</html>

Try to make your page descriptions engaging to the end user as well as optimizing for search engines. Remember that this, combined with your page title, is often the first thing a user sees of your website, listed amongst other similar listings, so make it stand out from the crowd!

Use less than 160 standard characters for your page description, and again try to integrate your targeted keywords. Try not to repeat your keywords too often (more than twice) and ensure it is readable and would make sense to a human reader who is less likely to click through to a site with a nonsense description.

Finally, remember to include a *call to action* within your page description, or something else to entice a user to click through and visit your website.

Page URLs

As you know, the individual pages and resources on your (or any other) website are accessed via a *Uniform Resource Locator* (URL), e.g. *http://www.yoursite.com/index.html*.

The structure of your web page URLs is an important factor for both human and search engine alike. Try to structure your directory paths and web page filenames to reflect the content of the web page, keeping them simple and short, while embedding some of your related targeted keywords.

Example: Optimized static page URL;

www.bobsparts.com/mx5-1999-mirror.html

Example: Optimized directory URL;

www.bobsparts.com/mx5/1999/mirror/

Shorter URLs tend to perform better than longer ones so keep them short and relevant, while at the same time including your required keywords. URLs should be all lower case, and so should your filenames. Use a hyphen (-) character as a separator between your keywords and avoid using other special symbols in your URLs.

Also ensure that your URL will make sense to a human reader, while including relevant keywords for the page. As with previous items covered so far, search engines also use the information embedded in your URLs to help classify the topic of the page, or group of pages within a directory, and so you should optimize your URLs before moving on further with your SEO tasks.

Site Navigation

Good navigation of your website is important in helping your visitors quickly find what they want. It can also help search engines understand what content is important to your website.

Your website navigation should be easy to understand and based on a hierarchy, starting at your home (root) page. Try to group similar items in a tree like formation, ideally with no page any further than 3 clicks away from your home page.

There is some evidence to suggest that text links are given more weight as a ranking factor than image links and so it stands to reason that the same would apply to links within your website navigation.

Use text links to create your menu(s) and use relevant keywords associated with the target page as the anchor text as opposed to generic terms like 'Home'.

Again, it is important to strike a balance here between using search engine optimized text, while still providing a quality experience for your website end user.

Search engines are not very good at reading *JavaScript*, and cannot understand *Java Applets* or *Flash* components. While it cannot be disputed that these technologies bring a new dimension to web pages, they do not suit our purposes with regard to fine tuning of our website for search engines.

Given the weight placed upon navigation as a ranking factor, it is suggested that you avoid the use of these (and similar) technologies in respect of your website navigation.

It would seem that at least one major search engine frown a little upon suicidal links, that is to say, links on a page that link to the same page, calling itself and going nowhere new.

This small quality flag is often triggered inadvertently by webmasters that copy a block of code containing the website navigation to all pages on the website.

All seems fine at first glance, but you will have added a link to some of your pages that link to the page in question. For example, your contact page may well contain a link in its own navigation bar to the contact page, causing confusion when a user clicks the link which simply reloads the same page.

Disable these types of suicidal links by removing the anchor tags that surround the clickable text part of the link, or by removing the link from the page in question altogether.

Unique Quality Content

Nobody likes a copy-cat, and the major search engines are no different. Unique content is favored over scraped or spun content, which can get your site penalized. Moreover, users know good content when they see it, and will naturally share your hard work by creating a buzz on social networks, forums and similar online communities if you deliver.

The days where content is king are over. Purchasing a bunch of articles from another website, slapping them up on the web and pointing a bunch of links at the site, will no longer suffice with the latest search engine algorithms. In fact the results of such actions will probably be counter-productive.

Only publish unique content that you have created yourself, ensuring a high quality with regards to content, grammar, spelling and accuracy.

When pushed on the point of *what makes a quality website*, the head of Google's web spam team stated that to qualify, a web page should bring something new to the web. Filling your web page with nothing but content obtained from other websites will not be enough to achieve high rankings, you must add some value of your own in some way.

Search engines seem to also favor content that is updated often, tending to index blog sites more often, but this is not always the case.

Some content is simply timeless and is not expected to change often. Other, more time sensitive content is more likely to be pushed down in the rankings by more up to date information.

Your keywords should appear within your content several times, spread evenly throughout the page, starting with your most important, and working them into the text in a natural sounding way.

You should also try to add variations of your keywords (synonyms) where possible, for maximum exposure.

Emphasize each of your main keywords *ONCE* within your text using bold formatting, via the *<b>* or *<strong>* tags, and then *ONCE* again, this time in italics using the *<i>* or *<em>* HTML tags.

Example:

This is a <b>keyword</b> in bold, but this <i>keyword</i> is shown in italics.

An excellent way to add new fresh content to your website on a regular basis is to add a *Blog* (web log) to your site. Posting regular blog entries will gain the search engines attention with new content at the same time as increasing how often your website is crawled and indexed.

A blog also offers the opportunity to interact with your customers on a more personal level, gaining further valuable insights into your customers needs.

Anchor Text

The text you use to link to other pages, the *anchor text*, plays an important role for SEO and achieving good rankings. When linking to other pages on your site try to use text links over images, and use keyword rich text that describes the page you are linking to. Try to avoid the use of generic anchor text such as 'click here', 'more' or 'home' etc.

While conducting Search Engine Optimization strategies such as SEO Link Building, it is easy for some webmasters to lose sight of how they use anchor text and the HTML anchor tag on their own website or blog.

Internal links, those pointing to URLs on your own website and external linking, where you link to pages on other websites, are treated very differently by search engines. Here we discuss both types of linking strategies to help you get your SEO and Links working together to improve your search rankings.

The use of text linking instead of images and buttons is the best choice as search engines seem to favor these types of links and give them more weight as a ranking factor. For this reason you should try to use text linking wherever possible, especially when linking to internal pages on your website.

Avoid the use of generic terms and phrases such as 'Home', 'Click Here', 'More' etc. Unless you wish to rank for these terms they serve little purpose with regards to SEO. You should strive to use related keywords within your anchor text, both for internal and external linking, both of which are described in more detail below.

Internal Anchor Text Linking

Anchor text for *internal* linking should always contain keywords related to the target page. Linking text containing two to three words seems to work best. Follow the same strategy for your website menu and site navigation links.

Only use related and relevant keywords that appear on the target page as opposed to the page containing the link. Try to avoid linking to the same page more than two or three times from the same web page as this can look spammy to search engines.

External Anchor Text Linking

SEO link building to external websites is still a relevant factor for your own website as search engines also look at the sites that you link out to when ranking your website. Again use relevant anchor text only.

We have seen some success in linking outward to other quality sites using our targeted keywords, but only link to well established, trusted, authority sites.

Linking to bad or unrelated websites can cost you ranking positions and in severe cases, such as linking to hacking websites etc., can get your site banned (sand-boxed).

It is also a good idea when external linking, to open the URL in a new browser window to ensure you do not lose your user if they click the link. Use the Target value of the anchor tag to specify "*_blank*" as the target for the new page.

Optimize Images

Whilst major search engines cannot make much sense of the content of an actual image, they do however try to make sense of the information contained within the images *<img>* HTML tag, notably the text contained within the *alt* parameter and the *filename* given to the actual image file.

Example:

> *<img src="[image file]" alt="[description text]">*

Search engine crawlers will read the alt parameter of your <img> tags in order to understand what the image represents. You should include your keywords, especially with linked images, while trying to describe the image. A good strategy is to consider what you would likely use as anchor text for a standard text link and use that information for your image's alt parameter.

Try not to repeat the same keywords within a single alt tag and avoid duplicate alt tags on an individual page. Use unique text in your alt tags for all images but keep them limited to 3 or 4 keywords related to the containing page, however, it is important to remember, as with text links above, the keywords chosen should be appropriate for the target page if the image is used as a link.

Alt Parameter Example;

> *<img src="..." alt="MX5 Wing Mirror">*

Follow the same procedures for optimizing your image file names, separating individual keywords with the '-' separator where needed.

Filename Example;

<img src="mx5-mirror-blue.gif" alt="...">

There does seem to be some weight placed on the displayed *location* of images, with those shown at the top of a page given more SEO clout. Therefore, images containing your most relevant keywords should appear towards the top of the page, with images containing lesser value keywords following underneath.

With website performance becoming an established ranking factor it is also important to look at the number of images contained within a single page. Page load speed will be negatively affected by a large number of images, and in turn may have a negative impact on your site rankings. Keep to a reasonable number of images on a single page and ensure each image file has been optimized (compressed) for use on the web to obtain the smallest possible file sizes.

Avoid the use of very small images (e.g. 1x1 pixel image) and small transparent images as a means to inject more links or text (via alt tags) as this is seen as spammy by most major search engines and could cost you in your fight for higher rankings.

It should also be noted that a page full of images, but containing little or no relevant text, will not be considered of value to the end user and therefore unlikely to rank well.

Heading Tags

HTML *Heading* tags are used to structure the information on a web page to aid users find the information they are looking for. Search engines also use them in a similar way to help decide the topic or relevance of your page.

There are six sizes/types of heading tag, starting with the *<h1>* tag, the most significant, and ending with the *<h6>* tag, the least important.

Heading tags typically make text contained within them larger than normal on the page, a visual clue to users that this text is important and could help them understand about the type of content located beneath the heading.

Multiple heading sizes are used to create a hierarchical structure for your content, making it easier to navigate through your document.

Example;
...
<h1>1999 MX5 Parts</h1>
<h2>Near Side Wing Mirror</h2>
Here we have a near side wing mirror for a 1999 MX5.
<h3>Price</h3>
New: 99.99 Used: 49.99
<h2>More MX5 Miata Used Car Parts</h2>
...

As you might expect, search engines give weight to these tags on a sliding scale, with the *h1* and *h2* tags given the most weight. You should concentrate your main efforts within these two tags, ideally placed towards the top of the page.

Try to implement your main keywords for the page, where suitable, within your heading tags, with your main keywords embedded in the *h1* tag, secondary keywords in your *h2* tag etc. Only use a *single* h1 tag per individual page.

Remember these headings tags must also be readable using natural language and make sense to the human visitors of your website.

Other Page Content

This section may appear late in this checklist, but each of the previous areas of website content optimization covered so far require the presence of unique quality content on each of your web pages, and this content should also be optimized for search engines.

Content length is a factor that should not be ignored. On the one hand, a page with too much content may suffer from a search engine failing to index the entire page in addition to slow loading times and the potential penalty that follows. On the other hand, a page with little content is unlikely to be seen of as offering value to users of the internet. Your content should be at least 500 - 800 words and contain your keywords spread sparingly throughout the text.

Try to mention each keyword or phrase several times throughout your text, starting with your main keyword. For each instance of a specific keyword you should have one instance *bolded* (using the *<b>* or *<strong>* tags), with another instance of the keyword shown in *italics* (using the *<i>* or *<em>* tags), with at least one other instance shown in normal text. Use the same procedure with your secondary keywords. It is also a good idea to ensure some of these tagged keywords appear towards the top of the page layout.

Avoid the overuse of keywords within your text; ensuring additional relevant text is present, including alternative words for your keywords. If the ratio of keywords on your page is too high this can be seen as 'keyword stuffing' and cost you a spam penalty. If your page does not make sense to a human reader then it is likely your have overused your keywords.

Text located towards the top of the page seems to have more traction. Ensure each of your keywords is shown at least once *above the fold* (the area at the top of a web page visible to a user without being required to scroll the page).

The quality of your website in the eyes of major search providers may be judged based upon the experience you offer your users. Is your site easy to navigate? Supported on different browsers? Fast loading pages? Free of viruses or other malicious code? Contains quality, unique content?

Ensure the quality of your content with regards to spelling and grammar. These types of errors can cost you dearly, for example a badly spelled keyword will not help you rank for the correctly spelled version, and could raise quality flags against your site.

Proof read all of your content to ensure it is easy to read and understand. Perform a *spell check* on all of your web pages and correct any errors you find. The same rule applies to all titles, headings and descriptions for your site.

Create a Blog

Creating a blog (web log) for your website or business can offer numerous benefits, both to your customers, and in terms of SEO. An increase in rankings has been seen for sites where a blog has been added, and properly linked to from the main website, using the main domain of the site.

Example; *http://blog.domain.com*

To get the maximum benefit from your blog, first create at least 8 quality blog posts, containing at least 500 words each, and then keep posting on a regular basis to prevent your blog going stale. Optimize your blog pages using the same SEO methods as outlined in this checklist.

Search engines love blogs and you'll often see a stream of new traffic, if you remember to link back to your main site from your blog pages! Blog posts are an excellent place to insert more keywords into the mix, and if you create quality articles of value to your users you will be enticing them to share your content on other blogs and social networking platforms.

The creation of your own blog will also allow you to communicate with your visitors, leads and customers in a more conversational manner, leading to valuable feedback and insight into your customer's needs and current trends. Always use a friendly tone in your blog posts, avoiding hard sales and marketing statements, while encouraging your users to share, interact and participate in discussions related to the content of your articles, as these social interactions are serving an increasing role as a ranking factor in SEO.

Search Engine Crawlers

You may not want certain pages of your website crawled and indexed because they might not be useful to users if found in a search engine's results, or from an SEO stand-point, are not relevant to the topic(s) that make up the rest of your site (a contact or privacy policy page for example is unlikely to be relevant to your chosen topic/keywords). Search engines can be instructed to ignore pages, and not follow certain links. This can be achieved in two ways:

a) Robots Meta Tag

You can add a *robots meta tag* to any page on your website and it may contain any combination of the following values in a comma separated list;

NOINDEX, NOFOLLOW and *NOARCHIVE*

NOINDEX will prevent the page from being indexed (listed) by search engines.

NOFOLLOW will prevent the links on the page being followed by the crawler.

NOARCHIVE prevents the search engine from caching a copy of the current page.

Example;

<meta name="robots" content="NOINDEX,NOFOLLOW"/>

In the above example the page containing this tag would not be indexed, and the links contained within it would not be followed.

b) Robots.txt File

A *robots.txt* file is a plain text file that tells search engines whether they can access parts of your site. This file must be named "robots.txt" and be placed within the root directory of your website.

This file uses the *Robots Exclusion Protocol* to specify the parts of the site that may be accessed by the crawler. In the example below all resources except for those stored in the images folder are accessible.

Example;

*User-agent: ***
Disallow: /images/

Warning: Care should be taken when employing any of the above methods to restrict access to your web pages by search engine crawlers. Spending hours optimizing your titles and tweaking your text will not help if you have inadvertently instructed search engines to ignore an optimized page!

Using Sitemaps

While our thoughts are turned to how we can restrict pages of our site appearing in search engines, it is worth giving equal consideration to ensuring that search engines can in fact access and index all the pages we have worked so hard to optimize!

We can do this effectively by using a number of free *sitemap generators* to scan our completed website and create a special XML file called a *sitemap*, containing a list of links that we want to be crawled and indexed.

Once created, this sitemap can then be submitted to the search engines via your webmaster tools area to aid them in discovering the links or your site and indexing them properly.

You can also notify search engines about the existence of your sitemap from within your *robots.txt* file.

Example;

*User-agent: ***
Disallow: /images/
...
Sitemap: http://www.yoursite.com/sitemap.xml

It can also be worthwhile, for your visitors and search engines alike, to create a *human readable* sitemap, that is to say, create a page containing a well structured list of links to all of the pages on your website.

Links to your Website

While conducting website marketing online, you may see many references to *back links*, a link located on another external website that points to a page on your own website. These links back to your website are seen by search engines as an editorial vote in favor of your website and as such considered a major external ranking factor.

Building a good portfolio of quality website back links is essential to the success of any website and should make up a significant proportion of your SEO activities.

There may have been a time when buying thousands of bad quality links to your site would propel you to the top of the search listings. After several updates by Google it is now the fastest way to get your website punished, or perhaps even removed from the index altogether!

So is the use of back links for SEO dead? No. But now Google pays far more attention to quality, editorial links, than it does to spam blog comments and forum posts. In fact inbound links from some blog networks could get you banned from search engines and leave you with a huge link cleanup operation to undertake.

Back Link Quality

The total number of links pointing to any web page used to be a major ranking signal. These days it is fair to say that all links are not created equal and that SEO link building is now very much about link quality over quantity.

Major search engines look at the quality of the links pointing at your website as well as the number. Try to avoid using automated submission software and other similar link building tools as the use of such techniques could get your site banned, or at the very least your rankings penalized. We have reached page one for a website with less than 20 links, it really is about quality over quantity.

Do not buy links, as paid links for the purposes of gaming search engines is a breach of webmaster terms for major search providers.

Do not participate in any link exchange networks or similar artificial link building techniques as part of your website optimization strategy. Instead, concentrate on obtaining quality editorial links from established authority sites, within your niche, by creating great value and compelling content that other website owners and webmasters will want to link to and share on social networks.

Link Density & Diversity

Recent updates have penalized websites for the excessive use of keywords in anchor text for incoming links. Natural links, those created by other webmasters because they like your content, would not all link using the same anchor/link text and nor should you. Natural organic links would often be the domain name of the site only or perhaps a brand name, or even the classic click here. Try to make your links look natural in this way with a sprinkling of keyword rich anchor text. It is recommended when building your back links to restrict the use of your keywords in link text to less than 30% of the total links to your site, with the remainder being made up of your website name, website URL, your brand name, and generic terms (e.g. 'click here') in equal proportions.

Seek to obtain a good diversity in the types of website that link to yours including websites in the same or similar niche, social media sites, topic related discussion forums, relevant directories, and wikis. Links from educational sites with a '.edu' domain seem to be given a little extra weight by some search engines. Links from authority sites in a related niche are also of greater value for SEO.

While marketing your website online you may be tempted by ads promising you 1000's of back links to your website; these are the quickest way to get your site banned due to recent Google updates (2013) as they are gained using spammy techniques and usually of low quality. Aim for quality over quantity when it comes to link building for your online business.

Submitting Your Website

The internet is full of search engines and web directories ready to add your link and inject new life into the heart of your website by sending you free traffic. URL submission is the process of submitting your website URL for possible inclusion. This section provides some useful information for effective website submission,

How to Submit a Website URL

Before seeking out obscure web directories and search engines for site submission it is important to note that both Google and Bing offer website submission directly from your Webmasters Tools area. You should sign-up for, and take advantage of these search engine services before moving onto other URL submission tasks.

It is a good idea to make the distinction between web directories and search engines. Directory listings are usually provided by the submitter of the link, whereas search engines obtain data about your website by using software to crawl the pages of your site, often using your Title and Description SEO meta tags to add your link.

When submitting to web directories you should pay particular attention to relevance, ensuring you visit each directory manually to select the correct category for your website listing.

Use accurate and meaningful titles and descriptions that include your targeted keywords, where possible, during your website promotion activities. Don't forget to include a call-to-action in your description to increase click through rates.

Web Page Load Speeds

Currently a relatively minor search ranking factor (but a factor nonetheless), the speed that your web page(s) load for your visitors plays a huge part in your user experience and so page load speeds should be kept to a minimum.

Independent research has shown that many users will click away from a website delivering pages that take longer than 3 seconds to load, and so this figure would make a good maximum to work with. Both on-page and off-page factors may be effecting your page load times, or a combination of several.

Some potential causes of slow page load speeds may be;

a) Shared or unreliable website hosting service, or an overloaded web server.

b) Inferior server connection, server hardware or bad network management.

c) Large web page file size, or pages containing too many server-side included files (Scripts, CSS etc).

d) Large image file sizes, large number of images, or other large web page content that must be downloaded when the page is first displayed.

e) Pages with dead links to resources, images, scripts, or other support files.

f) Poorly written or unreliable server side scripts or web applications.

g) Shared or overloaded Database (DBMS) servers.

h) Overloaded or slow DNS servers.

i) Slow loading advertisements, social share buttons or other third party web page content.

Dealing in depth with these various website performance and setup issues is beyond the scope of this book, however for best SEO performance we suggest;

a) Use a reputable web hosting company for your website, ideally a dedicated server or VPS (Virtual Private Server) with a dedicated IP address for each website.

b) Use server side caching, where available, to speed up (cache) access times for frequently used pages.

c) Compress image file sizes using appropriate image compression/editing software.

d) Optimize CSS and JavaScript libraries into single files.

e) Split extra large web pages into separate topical pages.

f) Keep the total number of hyperlinks located on any one page below 100 and always strive for more standard text over anchor text on a page.

Authority Site Status

While you may have heard of *Google Page Rank*, largely based upon the number of external links pointing to a website, another very effective website optimization technique is to establish your website as an *authority site* within your niche.

There are no hard and fast rules to achieving authority site status as Google keeps these ranking signals under lock and key, but some worthwhile suggestions for achieving authority status include;

a) Obtaining a unique IP address for each of your websites.

b) Ensure your IP address is not hosting sites that search engines may frown upon (bad neighborhoods).

c) Link out only to valuable content and articles related to your topic or niche.

d) Provide an inviting user experience, simple navigation and good page load times.

e) Avoid spam (often referred to as 'black hat') website promotion techniques.

f) Use on-page SEO in accordance with Google *best practices* and those contained within this guide.

g) Try to become a hub of valuable information within your niche or chosen topic.

Content Markup Ratio

A *quality* signal that may have some impact on your website rankings is the ratio of markup on your page compared to actual text content. A page containing a lot of embedded styles and formatting (using the <style> tag to embed CSS for example), and excessive use of embedded JavaScript may cause an excessive loading time for a page that offers little quality content.

When stacked up against another website whose page offers similar content, without the page load time issue, the latter is likely to prevail and appear above your page in search results.

Reduce your page load times by combining all of your JavaScript libraries (where used) into a single .js file rather than calling numerous files when the page loads.

Also try to replace all internal embedded formatting with CSS (cascading style sheets), and again place them into a single .CSS file. The overall goal here is to reduce the total amount of formatting contained within the text of your page, while at the same time reduce the number of individual resources (files) that are loaded when the page first displayed. Most resources loaded within the <head> section of your page would qualify as this section is processed at the time the page is shown.

Compete & Compare

Look in depth at your *competitors'* website content, (the web pages and websites that appears first in the search result for your chosen keywords). Watch the search results to see which pages perform well for your target keywords consistently.

How does your competitor use these keywords and phrases on their ranking pages or as part of an SEO strategy? How are their links and text structured? How much information do they offer and in what formats? Does your site use a similar structure?

There are various free SEO tools available on the web that allows you to analyze your competition, and view results along-side your own websites results. It is recommended that you take full advantage of these resources.

While looking into your competition is a good idea to turn your attention to your actual business model and how it stands up against the products and services offered by your competitor.

Do you offer good value for money? Search engines are getting smarter, and offering a competitive price can often get your site featured in results where others are ignored, for example, when searching for a book title a search engine may well suggest the cheapest current product offered on Amazon. This trend is likely to continue to grow in the future as search engines continue to develop more semantic algorithms in an effort to increase the quality of search results to the end user.

Website IP Address

The IP address of your website can impact your rankings to a varying degree. The worst type of penalty could be applied to a website that shares an IP address with another site that has been previously identified as hosting viruses or other types of malicious software. A lesser penalty could be applied to a site that shares an IP address with many other websites.

In terms of SEO and avoiding these potential penalties it makes sense to obtain a unique IP address for each of your sites. Most web hosting providers will offer these as an additional service on shared hosting, VPS and dedicated server packages.

To ensure your website always performs well it is recommended that you opt for the dedicated resources offered by virtual and dedicated server packages, over those of shared hosting services that may suffer from serious performance problems at busy times.

Legal Matters

There are a number of *laws and regulations* governing the conduct of business on the Internet, privacy laws and other regulation that should be complied with during the operation of your day to day business.

Whilst business law is beyond the scope of this book, some aspects do hold some direct significance with regards to our SEO efforts and so we cover those here.

Legal Compliance

It is important for your business, and website, to comply with international and local laws, not just from a legal stand point but as an SEO quality issue also. Search engines may expect to find certain compliance issues to be dealt with on your website, and penalize your site if not compliant. One example where this could be an issue would be with a site based in the UK that stores private data in cookies. A law in the UK requires websites that use such cookies to obtain permission from the user, failure to do so could be seen as a site quality issue by search engines.

Copyright has become a big issue on the Internet in recent years and the use of copyrighted material on your website is another possible indicator of bad quality. A page full of unique quality images is likely to rank far better than a page containing copied material picked up on the internet. Furthermore, copyright complaints about your site sent directly to Google can cause you to hit a severe penalty until the offending material is removed from your site.

Terms & Privacy Policy

Another potential quality issue that is sometimes overlooked by webmasters is to provide a clear and easy to understand privacy policy. Whilst this is not a legal requirement, it is an expectation of any legitimate business operating a website to supply such details in an open manner.

You should also have a page dedicated to your terms and conditions of use for your website, alongside any other terms or conditions related to the purchase or use of your products, service or business.

Terms & Privacy Templates

We have created several templates that can be used to create your privacy and terms of use pages that you may edit to suit your particular needs. However, nothing beats good business legal advice, and so obtaining the services of a lawyer with regards to the content of such pages is encouraged. You can find a link to these free templates in the *Useful Resources* appendix towards the end of this book.

AVOIDING PENALTIES

Black Hat Hurts!

The days of using automated software, to post thousands of blog and forum comments containing your keyword heavy website link, in order to game search engines and increase rankings are over. With the coming of Google's *Penguin* and *Panda* updates the days of SEO ranking for low quality links have come to an end, along with another form of web spam, namely keyword stuffing.

Keyword stuffing is the practice of using an unusual amount of related, or in some case, not related keywords, that are placed onto a page simply in an attempt to rank for those phrases.

Today, these types of *Black Hat* website promotion techniques will at best do you no good, and at worst get your website banned from the search engine altogether!

To avoid the wrath of the search engines, use keywords in moderation only, keeping them in context, and only seek links from quality sources and authority site. We have ranked websites recently with less than 20 links; it's all about quality not quantity of inbound links.

Never use unrelated keywords in an attempt to drive more traffic to your website. Search engines will notice this, and take action against you, leaving you not ranking well for either the out of place, or your targeted keywords. Only ever target keywords directly related to the topic or niche of the page.

Common Mistakes

While promoting your website or business there may be a number of mistakes that can be made with your online marketing that can directly affect the success of your business or internet enterprise.

Some mistakes can be caused by technical errors, others may be human error, or perhaps in some cases, as a result of bad promotion or SEO advice. In this section we explore some of the more common mistakes made by webmasters that could have a negative impact on your search engine rankings.

1: Low Quality Website Design

Your website is your business home on the internet. It is where you meet and interact with new potential customers. It is the one place where you must make your website visitors feel 'at home', quite literally. This should be the number one aim or goal of your website marketing online strategy.

Of course, you are a business that sells something, but merely selling your products or services without delivering a memorable customer experience for your visitors is a recipe for disaster. You need to ensure that every visitor to your website / online store remembers your brand, and your website, long after they leave your site.

Online business owners sometimes make the mistake of forgetting the importance of designing a website that reflects trust and professionalism. In a bid to spend less time, money or both, they end up with a website that makes little sense to the customer. Therefore, resist the temptation to save a few days or dollars, go for a quality website design that promises to deliver this message, while remaining straightforward and easy for your visitors to use.

2: Lack of effective SEO

Some business owners may also believe that once they develop and launch a website, they are now free of worries and visitors will flow to their website or online store without putting in any extra effort. They may forget that stiff competition and the search results rankings play a major factor in online success and require constant attention and review.

Without making people aware of your existence in the market you cannot attract them as new customers. This is where SEO Search Engine Optimization plays a critical role. While some may claim that Internet marketing is not something you can do by yourself, we believe even the smallest online business can perform many of the required tasks as opposed to a professional SEO to take on the job of promoting your website and attracting a steady flow of new visitors.

If you do decide to rely on an SEO company or agency check that it has a reputation for working on business websites, delivering results within an acceptable time-frame and using techniques that do not breach the search engine webmaster guidelines.

3: Duplicate Content Problems

Another online marketing mistake often overlooked by webmasters is the issue of duplicate content. Major search engines will list fresh unique content above stale, copied or duplicate content. Whilst this suggests that you should avoid stealing parts of other people's websites (scraping), it also extends to copying large blocks of your website to every page. Your navigation bars, header and footer etc are ok but avoid duplicating text in the actual content area of the web page.

Secondly, we have the problem of multiple names for the same piece of content. Is your website home page accessible using multiple URLs, e.g. *domain.com*, *www.domain.com* and *domain.com/index.html* variants? If so it is vital that these be setup the right way to avoid search engines seeing this as two (or more) duplicate websites, affecting the search engine rankings of all the pages involved.

The correct way to perform this is with the use of a *'301 Moved Permanently'* server *redirect,* whereby one location redirects the users browser to a single URL. For example; redirect all home page requests to www.domain.com no matter what variant is used. You should also redirect calls to your home page by its file name, for example; redirect all requests for the page *www.domain.com/index.html* to *www.domain.com* - Check your web hosting provider for details on setting up 301 Redirects.

If you have dynamic web pages that can be accessed via multiple URLs you should use the *rel="canonical"* tag to specify a single URL for the page or resource. This tag is placed into the <head> section of your page and takes the following form;

<link rel="canonical"
href="http://www.domain.com/dynamicpage.asp?page=1">

4: No Blog or Social Media Presence

Social signals from social networking sites and blogs are playing an increasing role with major search engine rankings. In addition to creating a blog with great content to encourage social shares, you should consider setting up pages with the top social networks and linking to your pages from your website and blog.

Don't forget to include a link to your website on your social pages. We have seen an increase in rankings by adopting this cross linking marketing strategy.

5: Ineffective Call to Action / Closing Sales

The desired outcome of all marketing online is conversion, turning potential customers into actual customers. Business owners forget that without a good, clear and effective Call-to-action (CTA), all internet marketing efforts go in vain.

An effective CTA is just as important as having a good product or service. Unless your call to action initiates the desired action, your website is not going to generate leads or sell any products. Every CTA must resonate with the offerings contained on the page. Avoid using random CTA buttons or text such as 'Submit', 'Click Here', etc., instead, design related and clear calls to action that are effective and prompt website visitors to take the specific action you want.

6: Lack of Visitor Tracking / Analysis

Businesses may also suffer from a failure to implement and utilize *Analytic* and *Visitor Tracking*. Without using analytic software, it is impossible to track your web site visitors, identify which web pages are generating the most (and least) traffic, pages that produce sales and conversions plus other important visitor patterns.

This valuable insight into your website visitor behavior can be used it to identify the best pages and best performing sections of your website that generate the least or most traffic, sales, conversions, even track offer pages.

After reviewing this data you can make the necessary changes to badly performing web pages, or sections of your website, in order to attract and retain more leads and customers.

Google Analytics is a very popular free website analytic and tracking service that can be implemented into your website by simply adding some HTML code to each of the web pages that you wish to track.

7: Dishonest Practices

While conducting business online you might be tempted to adopt get-rich quick attitude. You may adapt various underhand techniques, including exaggerating facts and features so that the potential new customers are lured to buy your product or services.

You could publish fake testimonials and reviews, highlight features that don't exist, or promise something and deliver something else to increase your sales. This might work in the short term, when people discover that you are not being honest; you will have a lot of problems on your hands.

Do not opt for short-term gimmicks and tricks. Adapt a proper, long term internet marketing strategy. Promise your customers only what you can deliver. Online marketing is not about earning profits in the short term, it is about earning trust and building a reputation, which will ultimately lead to increase in sales in the long term.

8: Lack of Consistent Online Marketing

Internet marketing is a long term form of online advertising. It is a slow and steady, ongoing process, however business owners may sometimes lose their focus and interest in the tasks related to their internet marketing efforts. They get bored, busy, or become less faithful about internet marketing.

Webmasters and business owners must avoid this type of mistake. You must be consistent with your online marketing efforts in order to achieve effective and sustained results. The expectation that your product sales will sky-rocket within the first few weeks of your online marketing campaign is not a realistic one. It takes some time for people to become aware of your brand, product and service, especially when other brands are fighting for their attention on the internet.

Keep your focus on your internet marketing plan, avoid the online marketing mistakes shown above and your efforts and investment will pay-off, but only if you continue to promote your website and brand consistently.

9: URL Submission

Avoid making some common site submission mistakes that can cost your site in terms of SEO and search rankings by following the guidelines below:

a) Do NOT use automated submission software, services or tools for your website submission, this is often seen as spam. Instead visit each website in turn and manually submit your pages directly.

b) Add your link to each directory using unique titles and descriptions each time that make sense, but also contain varying combinations of your main keywords.

c) Only submit your website to web directories that are relevant to your site, topic, or niche in some way. An incoming link from a pet care site to a car parts dealer is unlikely to offer much value.

d) Duplicate titles and descriptions may look like spam to some search engines. Use different combinations of your keywords and vary the text for your descriptions.

e) Do not enter page titles and descriptions in all uppercase, or use strange and unusual characters.

f) Keep page titles less than 60 characters in length.

g) Keep page descriptions less than 140 characters.

h) Use only keyword tags related to your website. Unrelated tags are the very definition of spam!

i) Check your email account for confirmation links sent to you by the search engine or directory. It is therefore important to use a real email address. This can result in a lot of unwanted incoming emails so it is advised that you create an email address specifically for this task using one of a number of free email services available on the net.

j) Avoid submitting your website to web directories more than once. Be patient. Some directories can take months to review and allow your listing, but could send you to the back of the queue if you keep submitting.

k) Check the individual website submission policy before submitting deep page links, that is, links to pages within your site that are not your home page.

l) Check your submitted URL is typed correctly and presented in the format requested by the directory. In most cases this will be the fully qualified URL of your homepage; e.g. *http://www.yoursite.com*

ALGORYTHM PENALTIES

In this section we examine the specifics of the most important updates to Google's algorithm that could cost your website ranking positions, due to automatic penalties placed upon it.

If you have a website that has been around a while, you should double check that none of your previous SEO activities (or those conducted on your behalf) has not triggered a penalty, or indeed could in the future.

If you are developing a new site you should make yourself aware of these new rules and implement the recommended guidance into your development to avoid any such penalties in the future.

For further insight into the full history of Google updates and the areas targeted by each, see the appendix at the end of this book, *Google Update History*.

Panda Update

Google Panda is a *significant* change to Google's search ranking algorithm that was first released in February 2011. The change is focuses on lowering the rank of *low-quality* websites (or *thin sites*), and return the higher-quality sites nearer to the top of the search results.

Some providers reported a surge in the rankings for news related websites and social networking sites, and a drop in rankings for sites containing large amounts of advertising.

This update was reported to have affected the rankings of almost 12 percent of all search results, one of the widest reaching updates to date.

Soon after the Panda update rollout, Google's webmaster forum became filled with complaints of scrapers/copyright infringers getting better rankings than the sites containing the original content, and at one point, Google publicly asked for data points to help detect scrapers.

Panda has received several updates since the original rollout, and the effect went global in April 2011. To help affected website owners and publishers, Google provided an advisory on its blog, giving some clear direction for self-evaluation of a website's quality. They have provided a list of points on its blog answering the question *"What is a high-quality site?"*, designed to help webmasters peek into Google's mindset.

Panda was a significant algorithm update that used artificial intelligence in a more sophisticated and scalable way. *Human* quality testers rated thousands of sites based on various aspects of quality, including site design, trustworthiness, website speed, and whether or not they would return to the website. Google's new machine-learning algorithm was then used to look for similarities between websites people found to be high quality and low quality.

Many new ranking signals have been introduced to the Google algorithm as a result, while older, less intelligent ranking factors such as PageRank have been downgraded in weight as a ranking signal.

Panda is updated from time to time and the algorithm is run on the Google network on a regular basis. In April 2012 the Google *Penguin* update was rolled-out, affecting a further 3.1% of all English search queries.

In September 2012, a Panda update was confirmed by Google via its official Twitter page, where it announced; *"Panda refresh is rolling out - expect some flux over the next few days. Fewer than 0.7% of queries noticeably affected"*.

Another Panda update was released in January 2013, affecting about 1.2% of English queries.

Panda vs Previous Algorithms

Google Panda affects the ranking of an entire website, or even a specific section of a site, as opposed to targeting specific individual pages.

In March 2012, Google updated Panda and stated that they were deploying an "*over-optimization penalty*," in order to level the playing field.

Panda Recovery

Google says that it only takes a few pages on a site containing poor quality or duplicative content to hold down your rankings (and traffic) on an otherwise good quality site, and recommends such low quality pages be removed from the site, blocked from being indexed by the search engine, or rewritten, and must be of a sufficiently high quality, as such content brings "additional value" to the web.

Website content that is broad or general, non-specific, and not substantially different from what is already available on the web should not be expected to rank well: Those sites are not bringing any additional value.

The key to recovery here seems obvious; fill our websites with fresh, unique and high quality content that has not been begged, borrowed or stolen from elsewhere. Bring something new by adding value in some way with unique insights, reviews, related facts and resources.

Prevent all pages that do not offer such high quality content from being indexed by search engines using meta tags in your pages, or a robots.txt file.

Penguin Update

Penguin is a Google algorithm update that was first announced in April 2012. Aimed at decreasing search engine rankings for websites that violate Google's *Webmaster Guidelines,* by using black-hat SEO techniques designed to artificially increase the ranking of a webpage, by manipulating the number of incoming links pointing to the page. These tactics are often described as link schemes or link networks.

By Google's own estimates, the Penguin update affects approximately 3% of search queries in English, about 3% of queries in languages like German, Chinese, and Arabic, and an even bigger percentage of sites within "highly spammed" niches.

In May 2012, Google rolled-out another Penguin update, Penguin 1.1. This update was predicted to affect less than one-tenth of a percent of all English searches. The principle goal for the update was to penalize websites found to be using manipulative techniques to achieve high rankings.

The purpose for Google was to catch excessive spammers, but it seems that some legitimate websites may have been caught with this latest algorithm change.

A few websites lost search rankings on Google for specific keywords during the *Panda* and *Penguin* rollouts. It appears anchor text was to blame in many of these cases, as the links pointing to these sites concentrated on only several specific keywords. While the content of the websites may have been satisfactory, as the update focused heavily on the quality of incoming links, the overall impact varied for different websites.

Google specifically mentions that doorway pages, those pages that are only built to attract search engine traffic, are against their webmaster guidelines. Regardless of this, many people still use this technique to target additional keywords, but should be mindful that Google has this technique clearly in its sights for action.

Penguin 3 was released in October 2012 and affected 0.3% of queries. Matt Cutts, leader of Google's web spam team, announced on May 10, 2013 that the next major Penguin update would sport the name Penguin 2.0.

Penguin vs Previous Algorithms

Before *Penguin*, Google released a series of algorithm updates called Panda (see previous section) with the first appearing in February 2011. Panda aimed at lowering the ranking of websites that provided poor user experience. The algorithm implements a system by which Google's human quality raters determine the quality of a website.

In January 2012, the *Page Layout Algorithm* update was released, targeting websites with little content, or too much advertising above the fold (the area of a web page that can be viewed without scrolling).

The strategic goals that Panda, Penguin, and the Page Layout updates all share is to bump up and display higher quality websites at the top of Google's search results. However, sites that were down-ranked as the result of these updates have different characteristics.

Two days after the initial Penguin update was rolled-out Google delivered a feedback form, designed for two type of users; those who want to report web spam that is still ranking highly after the algorithm change, and those who think that their site was unfairly penalized by the update. Google also has a reconsideration request form, available through Google Webmaster Tools for the 700,000 affected sites.

Penguin Recovery

Does your site use doorway pages to attract more traffic? It could be time to rethink think this strategy as you could be losing more traffic through a penguin penalty than you gain through the extra keywords. Replace these doorway pages with quality unique content that has some value, and target those pages to the extra keywords you need. Where adding fresh valuable content is not an option, these pages should be removed, returning a 404 response code to ensure search engines know this page no longer exists.

Do not bog down the top of your pages with lots of advertising as this leads to a poor user experience. Instead, place your most critical information (text containing your targeted keywords) as close to the top of the page as possible. Advertising should take up a secondary position on the page and not be excessive in number. Too many more than 2-3 ads on a page could start to cost you quality points.

When building incoming links to your site it is important to create a *natural* looking link profile. The overuse of your main keywords within the anchor text of incoming links will subject you to a penalty, and in some extreme cases, a manual action, or perhaps even the complete de-indexing of the site.

An ideal ratio for link anchor text is to target around a third of your links to use your keywords, another third should be your website or brand name, with the final third of your links using generic text such as click here, more etc.

If you have participated in link schemes, networks, or paid for links, you should start the task of removing these links, ideally at the source, but failing that, via the Link Disavow tool.

Concentrate on building high quality back links only from relevant, well respected, highly ranked, authority websites within your niche. The game is now about link quality and not so much about link quantity. Low quality links can actually harm your rankings, but it seems you do not need too many high quality backlinks in order to rank well.

Hummingbird Update

To celebrate its 15th birthday, Google held a press conference to announce the launch of a new *Hummingbird* algorithm update, claiming that Google search can now be a more humane way to interact with users and provide a more direct answer to a user natural language query.

Google suggests that its hummingbird algorithm has gradually abandoned the traditional model, allowing users a more natural ways to use search engines.. Google has said that this is the largest algorithm update in three years with the last update three years prior, the *caffeine plan*.

Google search engine can now make use of more complex search requests with a better understanding of human language, rather than a few scattered words. Google stated that such an algorithm improvement is necessary because the available data shows that many users enter a query in the search box to search the complete questions, to which Google wishes to return a valid result, e.g. answer the question.

Also as more and more Internet users access the web via smart-phones and tablet devices, they will often enter through a complete interrogative voice tool, in which the motive for this Google algorithm update lies.

There are two innovations designed to return the answer to the user, rather than to reflect a simple set of search results: The new engine has a better contrast filter - which can help users through mobile devices with Google to achieve a more natural conversation.

With the new filters, users can order his phone to "Tell me more about Impressionist artist information," Google can provide more background information such artist, genre, or other relevant or useful content.

In addition, the current design assumes a different intent role in the mobile space than within desktop space. Google promised to provide mobile search applications a "more unified design," and highlighted for the user to provide answers, rather than search results.

Google Now, with the emergence of the hummingbird algorithm, increasingly see themselves as an agent that can naturally interact with users, not just a portal leading to other websites. Google research and development department in the future may be more ambitious with its goals, perhaps providing medical diagnostics and personalized voting guide, or even "Why are we here?"

Hummingbird Recovery

This update does not really represent a penalty, but more an improvement to Google's search results, that could displace your site somewhat in the rankings. Certainly it would seem that we can improve our chances of ranking higher by developing two versions of our website, one for mobiles and optimized for the type of mobile search that hummingbird addresses, and our main website optimized for more traditional type searches.

MANUAL PENALTIES

Identify Manual Penalties

Previously, the primary focus of this book has been to provide the tools and information required to avoid any **Algorithmic Penalties** that could be placed on your website by search engines. Following the advice in this book should help you avoid any such penalties, and taking the corrective action outlined in previous sections should help you recover from these, once search engines have crawled and indexed your new website content and found the *quality links* that point at your site.

However, there is another form of penalty that could be place upon your site that will have a serious impact on your rankings, or perhaps remove you from the index altogether. This more critical type of sanction, a **Manual Action** by Google's web spam team, can spell the sudden death of a previously well ranking website.

If you have followed good practices, or have created a new web site based upon the advice presented so far in this book it is unlikely you will be affected by these issues, however there was a time when some of these bad practices were actively practiced by webmasters because they *did* produce results. Something that created a boost in rankings a year or two ago could be the very thing that caused your rankings to fall off the cliff into obscurity.

Readers who may have participated in such black hat techniques can use the information presented in this section to try and recover from a drop in rankings, but new webmasters should also review the information here in order to avoid falling into this very deep hole of obscurity.

Checking for Manual Actions

The first step to recovery is to identify; if a manual action has been taken against your site (as opposed to an algorithmic penalty), and the initial cause of this action.

The place to acquire this information is Google's Web Master Tools (WMT). You should already have an account, if you don't it is vital that you create one in order to monitor your traffic, and receive important notices about your website, including any manual actions that may have been taken against your site.

1. Visit http://www.google.com/webmasters/
2. Log-on with your username and password.
3. Select your website in the confirmed sites list.
4. Click *Search Traffic* in the menu on the left.
5. Select *Manual Actions* from the expanded list.
6. Review the supplied information.

Hopefully, if you have followed good practices, you will see the message "*No manual webspam actions found*". This indicates that there are no manual actions against your site.

If you are presented with any message(s) other than the one shown above, then you have a serious problem that requires immediate attention by following the steps in the remaining sections of this chapter.

Cleaning Up

Manual actions are very different from an Algorithmic penalty as a manual action is imposed directly by Google's web spam team, who constantly watch out for black hat techniques and will sanction webmasters who have employed any technique that falls outside of Google's webmaster guidelines.

Here we will examine some of the more common manual action notices that you may receive, the effect it may have on your website health (*symptom*), why you have been sanctioned (*cause*), and steps you can take towards a solution and recovery (*treatment*).

Common Manual Actions

"Unnatural links to your site"

Cause: Bad incoming links from irrelevant sites, other languages sites, spammy article directories, paid links, low quality directories, PR sites, and social bookmarking. Could also include; site wide links, link farms, reciprocal links, and 3 way linking etc.

Symptom: If you have received this notice from Google then the chances are high that your website traffic must have fallen from the top of a cliff, and in my experience these sites witness a drop in organic traffic, in some cases, of over 90%. This is one notice that no webmaster would like to see in his lifetime as it is one of the most difficult, and time consuming, to deal with and effectively recover from, leading to a prolonged period of massively reduced traffic.

Treatment: There is no quick fix remedy or solution for this type of manual action. You need to do a backlink audit by downloading all of the incoming back links from Google webmaster tools by selecting *'Links to Your Site'* in the *Search Traffic* section, and clicking on the *'more..'* link located underneath the area titled *'Who links the most'*. You will need to cleanup the bad quality links including; all irrelevant links, article links, paid links, low quality directories, PR sites, social bookmarking, site wide links and link farms.

You will need to contact the webmasters or website owners of these bad links and request that they remove these links. Follow up with an additional request in a couple of days if the link is not removed and send remainders.

Wait for around two weeks after your first link removal request date and then disavow all bad links using the Google disavow tool (see the next section *Recovery & Reconsideration*). After disavowing all of your bad links, send a detailed reconsideration request to Google. The entire process may take a number of weeks before you can expect Google to take any action.

Warning: Do not disavow *ALL* of your incoming links. If you do you will indeed have your penalty revoked, but your site will not get back the previous rankings and traffic it once enjoyed as not all of these links will be 'bad'. If you use a service provider for your SEO you should review and confirm the disavow file before submitting it.

"Unnatural links to your site-Impact sites"

Cause: This notice is given due to a pattern of unnatural backlinks, paid link networks, unnatural, artificial, deceptive, or manipulative links. This is a way of Google telling you that your participation in these types of link networks that pass page rank has been detected.

Symptom: Same as for *"Unnatural links to your site"*

Treatment: You may have purchased these links by yourself or perhaps hired an agency or freelancer to build links for you or do SEO. If you have paid for links you should consider removing them immediately.

Instruct your service provider (if you have one) to stop all link building activities and remove these problematic links.

After removing all paid links you will need to send a reconsideration request to Google explaining the situation, and the steps you have taken to remedy.

Warning: If any of these bad links generate real traffic to your website you should consider using a *"rel=nofollow"* parameter within the links anchor tag for those links. This parameter instructs Google to ignore this link and not allow page rank to flow as this is not an editorial link.

Example:

<a href="..." rel="nofollow">click here</a>

"Unnatural links from your site"

Cause: Selling text links on your website for the purpose of passing link juice.

Symptom: Sites are usually not affected initially but failing to take corrective action may lead to a 20-40% drop in your website traffic.

Treatment: Google is not against advertising as such, after all many sites rely on this type of revenue stream, but they do not tolerate the selling of text links that pass on link juice.

The solution to this notice is simple. Either remove the links from your site, or add a *"rel=nofollow"* parameter to the links anchor tag, preventing the passing of link juice, and the problem will be solved.

"Hacked site"

Cause: The website in question has been attacked by Malware, a Virus, a Trojan, or any other hack, including the hijacking of your page(s) or entire site.

Symptom: Doom and disaster resulting in almost 100% drop in website traffic.

Treatment: Replace the contents of your site with a valid backup, or contact your web hosting company who may be able to clean up the Malware for you. If your website gets attacked or compromised frequently you should consider upgrading your CMS or backend system to the latest version, or move to a more secure server.

"Cloaking & Sneaky redirects"

Cause: Cloaking is the practice of showing a different version of page contents to Googlebot than you would for a normal visitor in an attempt to trick Google with keyword rich content, while showing a lighter, more readable version to the visitor. The use of doorway pages can also prompt the issue of this notice.

Symptom: A 20-40% drop in organic traffic. The pages that employ the above cloaking technique will likely be dropped from the search engine index

Treatment: Remove the problem pages and create fresh pages with unique quality content. Use the "Fetch as Google" option in webmaster tools to check if the contents are served exactly the same to the end user as they are to Google.

"Hidden text and/or keyword stuffing"

Cause: Trying to cheat Googlebot with hidden text techniques in the form of hidden layers, divisions or by the use of camouflage (white text on a white background for example). This notice can also be caused by the excessive use of keywords only for the sake of optimization, and serving no benefit or value to a normal user.

Symptom: Affected page(s) or even the entire site may be de-indexed by Google.

Treatment: Check the keyword density of your pages and make sure keywords are not over 3-4% of your total text. Use the "Fetch as Google" and see if there is hidden content. Remove any offending content and send a reconsideration request (see next section).

"Pure SPAM"

Cause: Content that search engines consider to be useless junk; Spun content (an existing article that has been processed to use different words that mean the same, in an effort to make the article look unique to search engines), scraped content (content obtained from other websites), automatically generated keyword loaded gibberish, and translated content by automated tools.

Symptom: Usually results in a 100% drop in traffic.

Treatment: There appears to be no definitive solutions to this particular problem as these practices are considered the worst offences by major search engines and there is little chance these sites can earn the trust again.

However, before giving up completely and starting over fresh with a new website on a new domain, it would make sense to replace all of your pages with high quality, useful content, and submit a comprehensive reconsideration request. Even if your reconsideration request is successful you should prepare yourself for something of a wait while you earn back trust before expecting a return to your previous rankings.

Recovery & Reconsideration

Disavow Bad Links

Before using the *Disavow Tool*, you are expected to make every effort to have bad links removed on your own. Only after there is a "small fraction" of links left to remove, should one use the tool.

Google has made it clear that using the disavow tool is an act of last resort. They are looking to see that you put in at least as much effort into cleaning up a bad link profile as went into creating it. Simply dumping all of your links into a file and uploading it to the Disavow Links tool is unlikely to get the job done when used in this way.

Manual penalty recovery and Penguin algorithmic recovery are both appropriate uses of this tool. If you were hit by Penguin, and know or think you have bad links, you should probably use this tool.

When contacting webmasters to request the removal of a link, the most effective emails are personalized and don't require any thought on the part of the recipient. Let the webmaster know where the link is positioned on the page, the anchor text and where it points. By including those details, you will be perceived as human and make it easy for the webmaster to find and remove the link.

Warning: There has been a recent trend of webmasters demanding payment for a link removal. Don't do it. Simply document the demand for payment in your Disavow file as a comment and add the link address to be removed.

The Link Disavow tool is designed for SEOs and is not linked directly via webmaster tools. You can access the tool here:

https://www.google.com/webmasters/tools/disavow-links-main

Log into Google Webmaster Tools, then go to the Disavow Tool via the link above and select your domain from the list.

Clicking *Disavow Links* will produce a menu asking you for a file containing the links you wish to disavow. This is the list of any remaining links that you could not get removed manually. Upload the file and you're done.

Your file needs to be in plain text format (a .txt file) and encoded as UTF8 or ANSI7 format. Each entry should appear on a new line and either contains the full URL of the offending link, or to block an entire domain simply precede the domain name with the string '*domain:*'

You can also add comments to your disavow file by starting the line with a # character as in the example file below:

Example:

 # requests to remove links on this domain ignored
domain:needsblocking.com

 # no response to removal requests
http://www.somesite.com/page.html

 # domain demanding payment for link removal
domain:anothersite.com

Reconsideration Requests

Once all the hard work of link removal is out of the way and you're confident you have done as much as you can to remove bad links, it's time to submit a reconsideration request.

If you suspect your site has suffered some form of penalty but unsure of whether it's manual or algorithmic, submitting a reconsideration request would be your best way to find out. You can speculate, but why not just go to Google and ask? As with the disavow tool, there is no direct access via webmaster tools. You can get access to the reconsideration page here:

http://www.google.com/webmasters/tools/reconsideration

Only if you have suffered a manual penalty will you need to file a reconsideration request. When filing your request, here are some key points to consider:

- Be specific – Clearly state the steps you have taken to fix the problem and comply with webmaster guidelines.
- Confess everything – Do not attempt top hide anything, be honest.
- Accept responsibility – Explain why this issue will NEVER happen again, e.g. bad SEO advice.

***

APPENDIX A – GOOGLE UPDATE HISTORY

For those that wish to delve further into the world of Google updates that have been released since the company's inceptions, the list below presents a timeline of the most notable updates that should aid in taking on Google's mindset with a view to anticipating further changes to the algorithm in the future.

2013 Updates

Penguin 2.1 - October 4, 2013
Given the 2.1 designation, this was probably a data update (primarily) and not a major change to the Penguin algorithm. The overall impact seemed to be moderate, although some webmasters reported being hit hard. The Penguin 2.1 Spam-Filtering Algorithm Is now Live.

Hummingbird - August 20, 2013
Announced on September 26th, Google suggested that the new *Hummingbird* update rolled out about a month earlier. Hummingbird has been compared to *Caffeine*, and seems to be a core algorithm update that may power changes to semantic search and the Knowledge Graph.

In-depth Articles - August 6, 2013
Google has added a new type of *news result* called "in-depth articles", dedicated to more evergreen, long-form content. At launch, it included extra links to three articles within search results, and appeared across approx 3% of searches.

Knowledge Graph Expansion - July 19, 2013
Seemingly overnight, queries with Knowledge Graph (KG) entries expanded by more than half (+50.4%), with more than a quarter of all searches showing some kind of KG entry.

Panda Update - July 18, 2013
Google confirmed a *Panda* update, but it was unclear whether this was one of the 10-day rolling updates or something new entirely. The implication was that this was algorithmic in nature and may have "softened" some previous Panda penalties.

Multi-Week Update - June 27, 2013
Google's Matt Cutts tweeted, suggesting there would be a "multi-week" algorithm update between June 12th and the week after July 4th. The nature of the update was unclear, but there was massive ranking movement during that time period, although It appears that Google may have been testing some changes that were later rolled back.

Payday Loan Update - June 11, 2013
Google announced a targeted algorithm update to take on particular niches with notoriously spammy results, specifically mentioning payday loans and porn. Matt Cutts suggested it would roll out over a 1-2 month period.

Penguin 2.0 - May 22, 2013
The fourth Penguin update (named "2.0" by Google) arrived with only moderate impact. The exact nature of the changes was unclear, but some evidence suggested that Penguin 2.0 was more targeted to the page as opposed to site level.

Domain Crowding - May 21, 2013
Google released an update in an effort to control domain crowding and diversity deep within the result pages (pages 2+). The timing was unclear, but it seemed to roll out just prior to Penguin 2.0 in the US and possibly the same day internationally.

Phantom - May 9, 2013
In the period around May 9th, there were many reports of a phantom algorithm update. The exact nature of this update was unknown an un-announced, but many sites reported significant traffic loss.

Panda Update - March 14, 2013
Matt Cutts announced a Panda update at SMX West, and suggested it would be the last major update before Panda was fully integrated into the core search algorithm.

Panda Update - January 22, 2013
Google announced its first official update of 2013, claiming 1.2% of queries would be affected. A standard data refresh with no other significant changes.

2012 Updates

Panda Update - December 21, 2012
Just before Christmas Google rolled out another Panda update. They officially called it a " data refresh", impacting 1.3% of English queries.

Knowledge Graph Expands - December 4, 2012
Google added *Knowledge Graph* functionality to non-English queries, including Spanish, French, German, Portuguese, Japanese, Russian, and Italian. This update was stated to be "more than just translation", adding enhanced KG capabilities.

Panda Update - November 21, 2012
Google confirmed the 22nd Panda update, which appears to have been a data refresh only.

Panda Update - November 5, 2012
Google rolled out their 21st Panda update. This update was reported to be smaller, officially only impacting 1.1% of English queries.

Page Layout Update - October 9, 2012
Google rolled-out an update to its original page layout algorithm released in January, targeting pages with too many ads above the fold.

Penguin Update - October 5, 2012
After suggesting the next Penguin update would be a major update, Google released a minor Penguin data refresh, impacting only 0.3% of queries.

Exact-Match Domain Update - September 27, 2012
Google announced a change in the way it was indexing exact-match domains (EMDs). Google suggests that this change impacted 0.6% of queries.

Panda Update - September 27, 2012
At the same time as the EMD update, a fairly major Panda algorithm and data refresh update rolled-out, officially affecting 2.4% of queries.

Panda Update - September 18, 2012
Google rolls out another Panda data refresh. Changes to rankings were moderate but not on par with other large-scale algorithm updates.

Panda Update - August 20, 2012
Google rolled out yet another Panda data refresh, but the impact seemed to be fairly small.

7-Result Limit - August 14, 2012
Google made a significant change to the number of times a site can appear in the Top 10, limiting it to 7 results for many queries.

DMCA Penalty - August 10, 2012
Google announced that they would start taking action against, and penalizing sites with repeat copyright violations, most likely via DMCA takedown requests.

Panda Update - July 24, 2012
Rankings fluctuated for 5-6 days, although no single day was high enough to stand out. Google claimed ~1% of queries were impacted by the update.

Link Warnings - July 19, 2012
In a repeat of the March/April notifications, Google sent out another large number of unnatural link warnings via Google Webmaster Tools. Later, they announced that these new warnings may not actually represent a serious problem.

Panda Update - June 25, 2012
Google released another Panda update, but this appeared to be data only (no algorithm changes) and had a much smaller impact than the previous change.

Panda Update - June 8, 2012
Another Panda data update rolls-out, with Google claiming that less than 1% of queries were affected.

Penguin Update 1.1 - May 25, 2012
Google rolled out its first targeted data update after the initial Penguin algorithm update. This confirmed that Penguin data was being processed outside of the main search index, much like Panda data.

Knowledge Graph - May 16, 2012
In a major step towards improved semantic search, Google started rolling out *Knowledge Graph*, a SERP-integrated display providing supplemental object data related to certain people, places, and things. Expect to see *knowledge panels* appear on more and more results pages over time as Google strives to provide answers, not just links.

Panda Update - April 27, 2012
Barely a week after the last Panda refresh, Google rolled out yet another Panda data update. The implications of this update were unclear, and it seemed that the impact was relatively small.

Penguin - April 24, 2012
After weeks of speculation about an *Over-optimization penalty*, Google finally rolled out the *Webspam Update*, which was soon dubbed "Penguin." This update adjusted a number of spam detection factors, including keyword stuffing, and impacted an estimated 3.1% of English queries.

Panda Update - April 19, 2012
Google quietly rolled out another Panda data update. A mix of changes made the impact difficult to measure, but this appears to have been a fairly routine update and data refresh with minimal impact on site rankings.

Panda Update - March 23, 2012
Google announced another Panda update via Twitter while the update was rolling out. Their public statements estimated that this Panda update impacted about 1.6% of search results.

Panda Update - February 27, 2012
Google rolled out another post-"flux" Panda update, which appeared to be s relatively minor data refresh.

Venice - February 27, 2012
As part of their monthly update, Google mentioned the code-name "Venice". This local update appeared to more

aggressively localize organic results and more tightly integrate local search data. The exact roll-out date was unclear.

Ads Above The Fold - January 19, 2012
Google updated their *Page Layout* algorithms to devalue sites that are top heavy, with too much ad-space above the "fold". It was previously suspected that a similar factor was in play in Panda.

Panda Update - January 18, 2012
Google confirmed a Panda data update, although suggested that the algorithm hadn't changed.

Personal Search - January 10, 2012
Google announced a radical shift in search personalization; aggressively pushing Google+ social networking data and user profiles into the result pages. Google also added a new, prominent toggle button to shut off personalization.

2011 Updates

Panda Update - November 18, 2011
Another minor Panda data refresh with minimal impact.

Freshness Update - November 3, 2011
Google announced that an algorithm change rewarding *freshness* would impact up to 35% of queries (almost 3X the publicly stated impact of Panda 1.0). This update primarily affected time-sensitive results, but indicates a much stronger focus on recent content as a ranking factor.

Query Encryption - October 18, 2011

Google announced that they would now be encrypting search queries, for privacy reasons. Unfortunately, this disrupted organic keyword referral data, returning "(not provided)" for some organic traffic. .

Panda "Flux" - October 5, 2011

Matt Cutts tweeted: "expect some Panda-related flux in the next few weeks" and gave a figure of "~2%" affected by this update.

Panda Update - September 28, 2011

After more than month, Google has rolled out another Panda update. Specific details of what changed were unclear, but some sites reported large-scale losses in rankings.

Pagination Elements - September 15, 2011

To help fix crawl and duplication problems created by pagination, Google introduced the *rel="next"* and *rel="prev"* link attributes.

Expanded Sitelinks - August 16, 2011

Google officially rolled out expanded site-links, mostly for brand queries. Initially these were 12-packs, but Google appeared to limit the expanded site-links to only 6 shortly after the roll-out.

Panda Update - August 12, 2011

Google rolls out Panda internationally, both for English-language queries globally, and non-English queries, except for Chinese, Japanese, and Korean. Google reported that this impacted 6-9% of queries in affected countries.

Panda Update - July 23, 2011
Google rolled out yet another update. It was unclear whether new factors were introduced, or this was simply an update to the Panda data and ranking factors.

Google+ - June 28, 2011
Google launches a serious attack on Facebook with Google+. Google+ revolved around circles for sharing content, and was tightly integrated into products like Gmail.

Panda Update - June 21, 2011
Google continued to update Panda-impacted sites and data, and version 2.2 was officially acknowledged.

Schema.org - June 2, 2011
The three giants, Google, Yahoo and Microsoft jointly announced support for a consolidated approach to structured data. They also created a number of new "schemas", in an apparent bid to move toward even richer search results.

Panda Update - May 9, 2011
Google appeared to roll out yet another round of changes. These changes weren't discussed in detail by Google and seemed to be relatively minor in nature and impact.

Panda 2.0 - April 11, 2011
Google rolled out the Panda update for all English queries worldwide (not limited to English-speaking countries). New ranking signals were also integrated into the algorithm, including data about websites that users had blocked via the SERPs directly, or via the Chrome browser.

Google +1 Button - March 30, 2011
Responding to competition by major social networking sites, including Facebook and Twitter, Google launched the +1 button (directly next to results links). Clicking the +1 button allowed users to influence search results within their social circle, across both organic and paid results.

Panda / Farmer - February 23, 2011
A major algorithm update hit many websites sites hard, affecting up to 12% of search results according to Google. Panda seemed to crack down on thin content, content farms, sites with high ad-to-content ratios, and a number of other quality issues.

Attribution Update - January 28, 2011
In response to some high-profile spam cases, Google rolled out an update to help better sort out content attribution and limit the effectiveness of scrapers. Affected about 2% of all search queries, and a clear precursor to the Panda updates.

Overstock.com Penalty - January 2011
A public outing of shady SEO practices by Overstock.com resulted in a very public Google penalty. JCPenney was also hit with a penalty in February for similar bad practices.

2010 Updates

Social Signals - December 2010
Both Google and Bing confirmed that they now use social signals in determining website ranking, including data from Twitter and Facebook.

Negative Reviews - December 2010
After an article in the New York Times exposing how e-commerce site DecorMyEyes was ranking based on negative reviews, Google adjusted the algorithm to target sites using similar tactics.

Instant Previews - November 2010
A magnifying glass icon appeared on Google search results, allowing search users to quickly view a preview of landing pages directly from the result pages.

Google Instant - September 2010
Expanding on Google Suggest, *Google Instant* was launched, showing search results as a query was being typed. SEOs everywhere were most excited, only to realize that the impact was ultimately fairly small.

Brand Update - August 2010
Google started allowing the same domain to appear multiple times on a single result page. Previously, domains were limited to only 1 or 2 listings, or a single listing combined with additional indented results.

Caffeine - June 2010
After months of testing, Google finished rolling out the *Caffeine* infrastructure. Caffeine not only boosted Google's raw response speed, but integrated crawling and indexation in a much tighter manner, resulting in a 50% fresher index.

May Day - May 2010
In late April, webmasters started to notice significant drops in their long-tail traffic. Matt Cutts later confirmed that this was an algorithm change impacting long-tail keywords. Sites with a lot of thin content seemed to be hit especially hard.

Google Places - April 2010
Although *Google Places* pages were rolled-out in September of 2009, they were originally only an integral part of Google Maps. The official launch of a stand-alone Google Places; re-branded the Local Business Center, integrated Places pages more closely with local search results, and included a number of new features, including local advertising options.

2009 Updates

Real-time Search - December 2009
Twitter feeds, Google News, newly indexed website content, and a number of other sources were integrated into a real-time feed on some result pages. Data sources have continued to expand over time, including social media.

Caffeine Preview - August 2009
Google released a preview of a massive infrastructure change, designed to speed up website crawling, expand the

index, and integrate indexing and ranking in close to real-time. The timeline spanned months, with the final rollout starting in the US in early 2010.

Rel=canonical Tag - February 2009
Google, Microsoft, and Yahoo jointly announced support for the new *Canonical* Tag, allowing webmasters to send canonical signals to search crawlers and robots without impacting the human visitor experience. Use to prevent duplicate content issues by providing a single canonical name for the page.

Vince - February 2009
Many SEOs reported a major update that seemed to strongly favor big brands. Matt Cutts referred to *Vince* as a "minor change", but others felt it had profound, long-term implications.

2008 Updates

Google Suggest - August 2008
Google introduced *Suggest*, displaying suggested searches in a dropdown box located below the search box, as visitors typed in their queries. Suggest would later go on to power *Google Instant*.

Dewey - April 2008
A large-scale shuffle seemed to occur at the end of March and into early April, but the specifics were unclear.

2007 Updates

Buffy - June 2007
In honor of Vanessa Fox's departure from Google, the *Buffy* update was so named. Details are unclear, and Matt Cutts suggested that Buffy was just an accumulation of smaller updates and changes.

Universal Search - May 2007
Google integrated traditional web search results with News, Video, Images, Local, and other verticals, dramatically changing their format.

2006 Updates

Supplemental Update - November 2006
Throughout 2006, Google seemed to make changes to the supplemental index, and how filtered pages were treated. They claimed that the supplemental index was not a penalty, even if it sometimes felt that way.

2005 Updates

Big Daddy - December 2005
An infrastructure update (similar to the more recent *Caffeine* update), and rolled-out over a few months, wrapping up in March of 2006. *Big Daddy* modified the way URL canonicalization issues, resource redirects (HTTP 301/302) and other technical issues were handled.

Jagger - October 2005

A series of updates mostly targeted at low-quality links, including reciprocal links, link farms, and paid links. *Jagger* rolled out in at least 3 stages, from September to November, with the greatest impact felt in October.

Google Local / Maps - October 2005

After launching the *Local Business Center* in March 2005, and encouraging business owners to update their information, Google merged its Maps data in a move that would eventually drive a number of changes in local SEO techniques.

Personalized Search - June 2005

Unlike previous attempts at personalization, that required custom settings, the 2005 introduction of *personalized search* tapped directly into a users search history to automatically adjust results.

XML Sitemaps - June 2005

Google began to allow webmasters to submit XML sitemaps via Webmaster Tools, bypassing the more traditional HTML type sitemaps, and giving SEOs some direct influence over crawling and indexing of pages.

Bourbon - May 2005

"GoogleGuy" (most likely Matt Cutts) announced that Google was rolling out changes in search quality. It is unclear exactly what these changes were, but there was some speculation that *Bourbon* changed how duplicate content and non-canonical URLs were treated.

Allegra - February 2005

Some webmasters witnessed ranking changes, but the specifics of the update were not clear. Some believe *Allegra* affected the "sandbox", while others believed that *Latent Semantic Indexing* may have been tweaked.

Nofollow - January 2005

In an effort to combat spam, and control outbound link quality, Google, Yahoo, and Microsoft collectively introduced the *nofollow* attribute. Nofollow helps clean up un-vouched for links, including spammy blog and forum comments.

2004 Updates

Brandy - February 2004

Google rolled out a variety of major changes, including a massive index expansion, the introduction of Latent Semantic Indexing (LSI), an increased attention to anchor text relevance for links, and the concept of link neighborhoods. LSI increased Google's ability to understand synonyms and took keyword analysis and research to a new level.

Austin - January 2004

Google continued to crack-down on deceptive and unethical on-page SEO tactics, including the use of invisible text and META-tag stuffing. Some also speculated that Google placed the *Hilltop* algorithm into play, taking page relevance more seriously.

2003 Updates

Florida - November 2003
This was a huge and significant update that put updates on the map. Many sites lost rankings, and business owners were furious. *Florida* sounded the end for low-value SEO tactics, like keyword stuffing, hidden text etc.

Supplemental Index - September 2003
In order to index more documents without sacrificing performance, Google split off some results into the *supplemental index*. The down sides of having results end up in the supplemental index became a hotly debated SEO topic, until the index was later reintegrated.

Fritz - July 2003
The Fritz update was an infrastructure change. Instead of completely overhauling the index on a monthly basis, Google switched to a new incremental update approach. The index is now changing daily.

Esmerelda - June 2003
Esmeralda marked the last of the monthly Google updates, as a more continuous update process began to evolve.

Dominic - May 2003
The exact nature of the Dominic update is unclear, although the way Google counted or reported on backlinks seemed to change dramatically.

Cassandra - April 2003

Google cracked down on some basic link quality issues, such as massive linking from co-owned domains. *Cassandra* also came down hard on stealthy, hidden or camouflaged text, and hidden links.

Boston - February 2003

This was the first named Google update. Originally, Google aimed at a major monthly update, so the first few updates were a combination of algorithm changes and major data refreshes.

2002 Updates

1st Documented Update - September 2002

Prior to the *Boston* update (the first named update) there was a major change in the Fall of 2002. Full details are unclear, but this appeared to be more than the usual monthly Google Dance and PageRank update.

2000 Updates

Google Toolbar - December 2000

Guaranteeing SEO arguments for years to come concerning its relevance as a ranking factor, Google launched their browser toolbar, and with it, the Toolbar PageRank (TBPR) metric. TBPR is based upon the total number of incoming links to a web page, while taking no account for the quality of these links.

APPENDIX B – USEFUL RESOURCES

Some concepts examined in this book are examined in greater detail on our blog;
http://blog.ezwebsitepromotion.com

Our free templates to help build your privacy policy and terms of use pages can be found at;
http://www.ezwebsitepromotion.com/templates/

Visit the link below for a FREE SEO report. This resource will fetch, analyze your page contents, and return a handy report detailing on-page optimization issues that require attention in order to boost your website rankings.

http://www.spectralsoftware.net/seo-report/

Webmaster tools for the major search engines, where you can submit your sitemap and monitor traffic, keywords and other useful data are located at;

Google
http://www.google.com/webmasters/tools/

Bing
http://www.bing.com/toolbox/

Track your website visitors with *Google Analytics*, a free service providing valuable usage data and metrics.
http://www.google.com/analytics/

ABOUT THE AUTHOR

Darren Varndell began his career as a software engineer in the banking sector with a passion for personal computing. In the early 90's this passion grew to become his profession with the opening of his own personal computer store. In the two decades that followed, Darren's attention turned more to software development via the directorship of an Internet software services company. Recently, he has set out to help webmasters and internet marketers succeed online, by passing on his extensive knowledge of SEO (Search Engine Optimization) techniques that help boost website rankings and ensure a steady stream of free organic search engine traffic.

Unimpressed with the lack of straightforward, simple (and free) resources available to webmasters, and others hoping to succeed with Internet marketing, he started his own webmaster promotion website and Internet Marketing blog to help fellow webmasters obtain easy to understand SEO tips and advice that many SEO companies may not want you to know. Darren is the author of 'EZ Website Promotion', a series of Search Engine Optimization Publications containing extensive search optimization information and best practices, all available through Amazon.

Visit his website promotion and internet marketing blog located at: http://www.ezwebsitepromotion.com

If you have found this publication useful please recommend it to your friends and be sure to check out my other titles.

This book is dedicated in loving memory to Claire.

Other Books

DIY SEO & Internet Marketing Guide by Darren Varndell
http://www.ezwebsitepromotion.com/diy-seo-guide.asp

Provides an in depth look at effective SEO strategies, and Internet Marketing techniques, to produce better results for your website including; essential and advanced Search Engine Optimization, social media marketing, video SEO and other website promotion techniques.

SEO SOS by Darren Varndell
http://www.ezwebsitepromotion.com/seo-sos-guide.asp

This takes a tongue-in-cheek 'Fist Aid Guide' approach to common search optimization issues that could effect your search engine rankings, along with effective treatments to improve your overall website health, and avoid critical illness by way of algorithmic (Panda, Penguin etc.) and manual penalties. Use these simple but highly effective techniques to improve your website search engine rankings, boosting your website traffic, leads, and ultimately, sales

Future Publications
http://www.ezwebsitepromotion.com/seo-publications.asp

All books, both those listed above, and those yet to be written, will be made available via the link above. You can also join the FREE mailing list via the website for updates on future publications and releases.

Connect with the Author

You can connect with the author to provide feedback, discuss new ideas, get up to date SEO and marketing tips plus stay updated on new publications via the links below.

Website
http://www.ezwebsitepromotion.com

Blog
http://blog.ezwebsitepromotion.com

Facebook
https://www.facebook.com/ezwebsitepromotion.com

Twitter
https://twitter.com/ezwebpromote

Email
You can use the Contact Form located on *our website* as shown above.

You can also get the latest SEO tips and tricks sent direct to your inbox by joining my FREE mailing list here:

http://www.ezwebsitepromotion.com/newsletter/

FREE BONUS – Join our webmaster newsletter today and receive our '*Top 10 SEO Tips*' e-Book absolutely FREE!